Household Management

MARGARET WILLES

The National Trust

First published in 1996 by National Trust (Enterprises) Ltd
36 Queen Anne's Gate, London SW1H 9AS

© 1996 The National Trust
Registered Charity No. 205846
ISBN 0 7078 0241 5

A catalogue record for this book is available from the British Library

Text and picture research by Margaret Willes, Publisher, The National Trust

Designed by Peter Guy

Production by Bob Towell

Printed and bound in Hong Kong
Mandarin Offset Limited

Front cover: The kitchen at Lanhydrock, Cornwall
Title page: Tins in the housekeeper's store cupboard, Wimpole Hall, Cambridgeshire
Back cover: The scarlet baize door in the Staircase Hall at Uppark, Sussex

Introduction

The text for this booklet, and for its companion volume (see page 48), has been adapted and expanded from the National Trust's Desk Diary for 1996, which took as its theme the domestic arrangements in country houses. Here I concentrate on looking at how a country house was run through the centuries, the realms of the housekeeper, the butler, the cook and the nursery maids.

Our own domestic arrangements have become so streamlined and relieved by machines that it is hard to imagine what life was like one hundred years ago, let alone five centuries back. Keeping a house clean and running smoothly was the responsibility of the housekeeper with her housemaids – their hours were long, their tasks complex and sometimes backbreaking. Just imagine what it would be like to be one of the most junior maids in a large household, faced with piles of washing-up in a cold and damp scullery.

The feedback we get from visitors to National Trust houses is that they particularly enjoy seeing the kitchens, bathrooms and service areas. As most of us, if we were to be transported into the past, would find ourselves lugging the water up the stairs rather than wallowing pleasurably in a hip bath in front of the bedroom fire, the overwhelming feeling must be of gratitude that we live in such convenient times. But studying the way a country house was run provides an excellent insight into history precisely because we do have a common experience.

I have drawn on National Trust guidebooks and Trust knowledge to pull together all the threads of this book. Inevitably two houses stand out because they are such good examples of domestic architecture: Erddig in Clwyd, where not only the service rooms but also the household accounts are so complete; and Lanhydrock in Cornwall, where even the attic bedrooms of the servants have been restored to provide a vivid picture of household life at the end of the last century. Three books were particularly useful to me: *The Servants' Hall* by Merlin Waterson; *The Art of Dining* by Sara Paston-Williams; and *Home Comfort* by Christina Hardyment. I am grateful to them all.

The Housekeeper

With singular filial impiety, the novelist H. G. Wells wrote of his mother's tenure as housekeeper at Uppark in Sussex: 'The worst housekeeper that was ever thought of . . . she did not know how to plan work, control servants, buy stores or economise in any way. She did not know clearly what was wanted upstairs. She could not even add up her accounts with assurance.' Thrift, numeracy, organisational and management skills were all vital qualities for the ideal housekeeper to possess, as was discretion. This was another of Mrs Wells's failings: in 1893 she was sacked after thirteen years' tenure for gossiping about her employers.

In the Tudor period, when large households were staffed almost entirely by men – the laundry and the dairy were exceptions – female housekeepers could be found looking after the establishments of bachelors or widowers. But in the 17th century, as the ceremonial attached to the running of households disappeared and servants began to migrate below stairs, women servants became a regular feature – with the bonus that they could be paid less. At Cannons in Middlesex, home of the Duke of Chandos, a housekeeper is recorded in the early 18th-century accounts. Although she ate with the senior household officers, she earned the smallest annual salary: £10.

As the 18th century progressed, so the housekeeper rose in power, the female counterpart of the butler or the steward, formidable in her dark silk dress, the keys to the household at her belt. She supervised all the female members of staff except the lady's maid, nurse and cook, who were answerable directly to the mistress of the house. She looked after the household accounts and bought in supplies. Mrs Smith, housekeeper at Petworth in Sussex in the mid-19th century, kept a daily account book which gives a good idea of the bulk purchasing that was required: 54 yards of calico at a time, 96 knife cloths, 12 lb of cotton wool, 6 best mops (another 6 were bought 4 weeks later), 12 lb fuller's earth (for the laundry), ½ lb beeswax for polish, 12 lb salt butter, and so on.

It was often the housekeeper's duty to show visitors around the house. Kedleston Hall in Derbyshire, for instance, was open to visitors from the time it was built in the 1760s. The portrait of Mrs Garnett, the housekeeper, shows her holding a guidebook to the house's contents

The housekeeper's empire included not only the storeroom, the china closet and the linen cupboard, but also the still-room. In earlier centuries, this had been the room where the lady of the house would distil cordials and waters for medicine, cooking and general household use, and prepare the sweetmeats and other exotic dishes eaten as the final course of dinner, known as the banquet or dessert. By the 18th century the still-room had passed to the housekeeper, and with the help of a maid she prepared breakfast, made tea and coffee, and sometimes the nursery meals, supervised the washing of the finer household china, and made preserves and ices.

The housekeeper and most of the maids under her supervision were permanent fixtures, often looking after the house while the family was away. Mary Salusbury, housekeeper at Erddig in Clwyd from the 1780s, was the recipient of frequent messages from Philip Yorke I via the agent, John Caesar. A typical example is dated 14 November 1782: 'Your mistress would have Molly Salusbury look out her white negligee sack and the hoop she wears with it, also a pair of white silk shoes.' For twenty-four years, from 1744, Philippa Hayes was housekeeper at Charlecote in Warwickshire to George Lucy, a bachelor who was frequently away for prolonged periods in Bath, London or on the Continent. Their correspondence was long and close, with Mrs Hayes relating local gossip and asking Lucy to execute commissions in London, such as buying fine green tea from Twinings and paper for lining shelves, while he concentrated on details about his clothes and his health, two of his favourite subjects.

The housekeeper's room was her headquarters. At Erddig, Clwyd, this was sited strategically next to that of the agent, who ran the estate. An interlinking door could be closed when relations were not cordial. Within the housekeeper's room itself are ample cupboards for dry stores and linen.

Under the housekeeper came a whole hierarchy of maids. At the top were the upper housemaids, who undertook the lighter jobs, such as making the beds in the best bedrooms, keeping them clean and tidy, and keeping an eye on the lower housemaids. The latter would lay and light the fires, clean the living rooms, polish the brass, carry upstairs the water for washing and empty the chamberpots. Some maids had particular duties – in the still-room, the laundry, the dairy and the nursery. At the very bottom of the pecking order came the hapless scullery maid, often in her early teens, whose job was to keep the kitchen range clean, light it first thing in the morning, and to do all the mountains of washing-up.

Whatever their position, housemaids were expected to rise at 5am or 6am and work right through until late at night. Unlike the housekeeper, they wore uniform, print dresses for morning, dark dresses for the afternoon and evening, with white frilly aprons and caps. While the housekeeper might have a bedroom and sitting room somewhere downstairs, maids' rooms were usually up in the attics. At Erddig, the attic rooms are furnished as they would have been at the beginning of this century: two bedrooms and a workroom, where the maids could relax when off duty.

A maid's room on the attic floor at Lanhydrock, Cornwall. Here they could sew, knit and read. The male and female servants' rooms were separated by a connecting door, the key for which was kept by the housekeeper

Bell-pushes at Lanhydrock

Books of household management published in the 18th and 19th centuries attest to the complex and ingenious cleaning skills required. Susannah Whatman, who lived at Turkey Court in Kent, compiled a housekeeping book between 1776 and 1800. Because of the rapid turnover of housemaids in her modest household, she wanted to instruct new incumbents in the necessary routines. A typical entry runs:

> The sun comes into the Library very early. The window on that side of the bow must have the blind let down. The painted chairs must not be knocked against anything, or against one another. A chair must not be placed against the door that goes into Mr Whatman's Dressingroom. All the space between the daydo [dado] and skirting board is plaister. Therefore, if it is knocked, it will break. The books are not to be meddled with, but they may be dusted as far as a wing of a goose will go.

When the family was not in residence, the housekeeper and the maids would dismantle the rooms of state, and after cleaning would protect the vulnerable furniture. At Erddig, white cloth covers were put on chairs, walnut covers on glass-topped tables, and sprigged calico blinds over windows. This is a ritual still observed today at National Trust properties, with the Trust's housekeepers 'putting the houses to bed' at the end of each visitor season.

The Stone Corridor at Felbrigg Hall, Norfolk; its ghostly appearance has been produced by the house staff, who have put the house and its contents to bed for the winter

The Butler

Our modern image of the butler is a man of dignified mien, soberly dressed, and if P. G. Wodehouse's Bertie Wooster has anything to do with him, a look of disapproval frozen on his features. He is the pre-eminent male servant of the country house, unobtrusively carrying out the tasks that ensure its smooth running.

But where does this formidable character come from? He has a long and varied past. In the Middle Ages and the 16th century he was the yeoman of the buttery, a middle-ranking servant under the authority of the clerk of the kitchen. Buttery is the English translation of the French *bouteillerie*, or place of the bottle, and this particular servant was responsible for the beer and wine in the cellars, and their serving up.

In time, gentlemen servants such as the clerk of the kitchen began to disappear from the domestic scene, resulting in a rise in status for the second rank of servants, such as the yeoman of the buttery. Absorbing the responsibilities for the ewery (linen and plate) and the pantry (bread and candle store), the butler climbed towards his 19th-century eminence, addressed as 'Mr'. He was not, moreover, required to wear livery, the special uniform provided by an employer, usually picking out family colours to underline the dignity and status of the household. Instead, the butler wore 'gentleman's costume' of black suit and white tie.

Butlers, footmen and the chauffeur at Polesden Lacey, Surrey, in the 1930s. Mrs Ronnie Greville was a lavish giver of dinner parties, where guests were served by a brace of butlers, 'the conventional Boles and the communist Bacon' according to Lord Clark. Unfortunately history does not record which was which in this photograph

In Victorian country houses, the staff below stairs observed the concept of hierarchy just as much as the family above stairs. At the top of the hierarchy were the Upper Ten, which included the butler and the housekeeper. These upper servants would take their meals in the servants' hall, then adjourn to the housekeeper's room (p.6), known familiarly as the Pugs Parlour, for pudding and wine. The rest of the household, known for convenience as the Lower Five, remained in the servants' hall, sticking firmly to beer.

The duties and authority of the 19th-century butler echoed his earlier incarnations. If the household did not have a brewer, he made the household's beer. He enjoyed the perquisites of selling off empty bottles and candle ends (a reminder that the butler had inherited the role of yeoman to the pantry). He was responsible for the care of the wine and beer cellars: at times this could involve rising at 4am to decant the wine for dinner. He was also responsible for the inventory of plate and its care. Again, a reminder of a former incarnation, when the yeoman of the ewery would look after the gold and silver vessels on the buffet. His afternoons would be spent in the entrance hall, announcing callers, and checking that all was well with the ground-floor rooms, with fires attended to, blinds up, and so on.

The Yorkes of Erddig were neither great connoisseurs of their cellar nor very concerned about nice points of etiquette, so required other qualities of their butlers. One of the most successful seems to have been George Dickinson, butler to Simon Yorke III from 1869 to 1888. He helped Simon's children catch, chloroform and mount butterflies to exhibit in the Family Museum. By what Mrs Yorke succinctly describes as a curious coincidence, Dickinson died under chloroform during a minor operation in the house, and is duly commemorated by a hatchment in the servants' hall.

The servery at Lanhydrock, the essential link between kitchen and dining-room, and realm of the butler. The steel hot-cupboard, fuelled by the central heating system, is flanked by a butler's tray and the linen press. Clever planning enabled the butler and footmen to watch the servery as they stood by the sideboard in the dining-room, while the view was masked for guests at the table

Fire buckets hanging in a corridor at Lanhydrock. The house is full of deterrents to avoid a repeat performance of the disastrous fire of 1881

The control centre of the butler's activities was his pantry. Mr Coad, the butler at Lanhy-drock in Cornwall in the 1880s, presided over a pantry situated opposite the dining-room servery. Valuable silver was kept in the strongroom next door to the butler's bed-room, which led directly off the pantry. It is furnished with two lead-lined sinks to wash the dining-room china and glass, and a large wooden table to accommodate the wine assembled for the day's consumption. Bells summoned the butler to the various rooms, although in the sophisticated pantry at Cragside in Northumberland there is an internal telephone. In addition there is a Butler's Room, strategically placed so that when the but-ler was on duty he was within easy access of the front door, the kitchen, pantry and wine cellars, the dining-room and other reception rooms.

At meals, the butler would superintend waiting with his staff, the footmen. The mid-19th-century move in the style of dining from *à la française* to *à la russe* undoubtedly made this role more onerous. *A la française* had been the style practised since the Middle Ages, with all the dishes laid on the table simultaneously in two courses, the heavier foods in the first course, the lighter in the second – very much in the style prevailing in Chinese restaurants. The diners would help themselves to the different dishes, requiring assis-tance only in locating distant dishes and for drinks. With *à la russe*, dishes would be divid-ed into different courses, brought to the table by the butler and footmen in the style now practised at most meals both in the home and in restaurants.

The butler's pantry at Cragside, Northumberland. Among the equipment there are two portable stoves for shooting picnics on the grouse moors

Footmen had a varied history. Their name derives from their original role as attendants who ran on foot beside their master or mistress when they were out riding or in a carriage. Inn signs can still be seen showing the running footman, complete with a long cane containing a mixture of eggs and white wine to give him sustenance. In the 18th century the footman began to discard his running duties and, coming under the supervision of the butler, he took on a whole host of tasks within the house, from carrying coals up to rooms, to cleaning boots, trimming lamps, laying the table for meals, answering the front door and, at Erddig, sleeping in the butler's pantry to ensure nobody stole the family silver.

When footmen were still required to run, they represented a status symbol, sometimes being entered in running races against rival households, while their masters laid bets. This concept survived through to the 19th century, when footmen were hired for their looks and their legs – 'calves came before character'. At times they were matched in pairs, the taller ones being paid higher wages. Footmen, unlike the butler, wore livery: in the 19th century this meant that they wore the fashions of a hundred years earlier, with knee breeches and braided coats with shoulder knots. At Clandon Park in Surrey in 1876, Lord Onslow provided his footmen with silk stockings, gloves and pumps, and one guinea per annum to pay for powder to dress their hair for state occasions.

The livery room next to the footmen's bedrooms on the top floor at Lanhydrock. The livery in the wardrobes was made in 1904 for footmen, postilions and the coachman in the household of J.S. Tregoning of Landue, another Cornish house

Kitchens

In 1864 the architect Robert Kerr wrote in *The Gentleman's House* that the kitchen had acquired 'the character of a complicated laboratory'. To the Victorians, with their admiration for scientific enquiry, such a comparison would be high praise indeed. But the kitchen with its attendant service rooms had for centuries represented the bustling heart of the house.

Four hundred years ago, when most households still dined communally in the great hall, the kitchen was usually sited beyond the screens passage, along with the buttery and pantry. The kitchen at Buckland Abbey in Devon was built by Sir Richard Grenville in the mid-16th century as part of his conversion of the Cistercian monastery into a private house. The kitchen at Buckland would have been an all-male establishment, with the clerk of the kitchen in overall charge, and the cooks assisted by scullions, young boys whose tasks included turning the spits in the huge roasting hearth.

The cooks would have learned by word of mouth the skills of producing pottages, a cross between stew and soup, sauces for roast meats and fish, and crustades, rich custards in pastry cases. The first cookery book in English was not published until 1572; even then it would have been unlikely that many cooks could read. In the last years of the century a whole series of cookery books was produced, with titles like *The Good Huswives Handmaid for Cookerie in her Kitchin* of 1597. These were aimed at the wives of newly rich merchants, anxious to keep up with the latest culinary fashions.

The Tudor kitchen at Buckland Abbey, Devon. In front is a stout wooden table, behind, the roasting hearth with spits and remains of the complex pulley system for storage of food

By the mid-17th century most families had withdrawn from the great hall, preferring to dine in the privacy of the great chamber or parlour. The architect Sir Roger Pratt, returning from exile on the Continent at the Restoration in 1660, urged that new-built houses should have their ground floor raised to add height and majesty, and to supply a 'very good story' below for domestic offices. The kitchen at Ham House, Surrey, installed by the Duke and Duchess of Lauderdale in the 1670s, follows this precept. The Lauderdales were leading figures at the Stuart court and up with the latest fashions. Their head cook was a Frenchman, John Blangy, who commanded an annual salary of £20, on a par with that of the steward. Women were making their appearance in the country-house kitchen, albeit in a menial capacity: Blangy had two kitchenmaids, Mary Trever and Grace Phyllips, each earning a salary of £3 10s.

Stewing hearths had been introduced to Ham to cook the fashionable French 'made dishes' such as fricassés – cold mutton chopped small and fried in sweet butter with wine and spices. The kitchen of the prosperous Cumbrian farmers, the Brownes, at Townend is of the same date as Ham, but reflects a more conservative way of life. Nevertheless Elizabeth Birkett, who married Benjamin Browne in 1702, includes in her commonplace book of recipes medical, domestic and culinary, a recipe for 'Scotch Collops' after the French fashion.

A range of printed cookery books was now available, including *The Accomplisht Cook*, published in 1660 and addressed primarily to professional cooks and 'approved by the 55 years' experience and industry of *Robert May* in his attendance on several persons of great honour'.

The 17th-century kitchen or down house at Townend, Cumbria. The fitted oak furniture was gradually installed by the Browne family to make maximum use of the room

The Georgians often built their kitchens away from the main body of the house, partly as a precaution against fire, partly to remove cooking smells and noises offensive to the sensibilities of the family. At Uppark the kitchens, built in the 1690s in the Pratt-approved style in the basement, were removed in the early 19th century to a detached wing, connected to the house by an underground passage. This inconvenient outpost was abandoned at the end of the century, when the kitchen returned to its original site. At Erddig, Philip Yorke I's fear of fire caused him to move the kitchen into a separate building in 1770, while an actual fire in 1778 induced John Parker to do the same at Saltram in Devon.

Although very fashionable households still had a male cook, such as Carême, the great French chef who held sway in the Prince Regent's kitchen at the Royal Pavilion in Brighton, most country-house cooks were now women. They may well have been inspired by a series of books published by women: Eliza Smith, *The Compleat Housewife*, 1727; Hannah Glasse, *The Art of Cookery made Plain and Easy*, 1747; Elizabeth Raffald, *The Experienced English Housekeeper*, 1769; and Mary Smith, *The Complete Housekeeper*, 1772. The last, written by the former housekeeper to Sir Walter Calverley Blackett at Wallington in Northumberland, included seasonal menus which made a feature of the delicate vegetables and fruit that could now be supplied from the garden hothouses. No fashionable dessert course was served without ices, which could be made on the premises if the estate had an ice-house, or bought in from confectioners. Pineapple moulds were particularly popular because the fruit was such a symbol of luxury.

The Great Kitchen at Saltram, Devon, built by John Parker in a separate building following a fire in 1778. The kitchen was provided with the most up-to-date equipment, including candle lamps and a splendid batterie de cuisine. The roasting range dates from 1810, while the free-standing kitchiner was installed later in the century

The kitchen and service rooms at Lanhydrock, rebuilt following a disastrous fire in 1881 that destroyed most of the house, are modelled almost exactly on Kerr's laboratory principles (p.20). The kitchen is situated far enough from the dining-room to ensure cooking smells did not intrude, but close enough for the food to arrive on the table hot – only made possible with the replacement of the dining style *à la française* by *à la russe*. Around the kitchen, which is as spacious as a medieval dining hall, are laid out the related departments: the scullery, bakehouse, dry larder, fish larder, meat larder and the dairy.

In the 1880s this splendid complex was the domain of the cook, Mrs Wes Coad, who supervised a staff of ten. Mrs Coad would have needed all these support staff, for she had to produce three, and possibly four, substantial meals a day. In addition, she would be expected to provide nursery meals for the growing number of Clifden children, and cater for cricket teas, croquet parties, picnics, tenants' suppers, and other celebrations. To guide her was a plethora of cookery books. The most famous and most popular were Eliza Acton's *Modern Cookery Book*, 1845, and Mrs Beeton's *Book of Household Management*, which first appeared in 1861. But these books were written for middle-class households keen to follow the trends set by their social superiors. More appropriate for the Lanhydrock cook was Charles Elmé Francatelli's *Cook's Guide* published in 1862. With the help of Francatelli, a formidable *batterie de cuisine* and her 'complicated laboratory' of larders and service rooms, she could summon up the dishes of artifice and complexity so admired by the Victorians.

The kitchen at Lanhydrock, built in 1883 on the scale of an Oxbridge college dining hall. The clerestorey windows can be opened by a system of shafts and gearings connected to handwheels in the end dresser

Dairies

In the Middle Ages and the 16th century, products of the dairy, such as milk and butter, were regarded with a certain amount of suspicion. Fresh milk 'engendered wind in the stomach', so was a drink most suitable for children, the old and the infirm. The recommended time for the consumption of butter was the morning because of its laxative qualities. It was regarded as unwholesome for grown men to eat it from midday onwards.

These attitudes went out with the Stuarts – indeed this was regarded as 'the golden age of butter' when it was used extensively in cooking. With the increasing vogue for foreign dishes, cheese too represented an important ingredient. In the 18th century, dietary favour combined with romantic arcadian concepts to produce the fine 'fancy dairies' that were attached to country houses.

At Shugborough in Staffordshire, the very attractive dairy started life as a banqueting chamber, designed for the Anson family in the 1760s by James 'Athenian' Stuart on the model of the Tower of the Winds in Athens. Originally it was surrounded by a lake, but in 1805 the lake was drained and the tower converted into a dairy by Samuel Wyatt. The lowest section was the working dairy, with cows led along a sunken track from the home farm to be milked in the brick stalls around the base. The dairy itself is lined with slate, and has thick stone shelves and arched vaults.

Above is the 'fancy dairy', where Lady Anson and her friends could adopt the role of dairymaids in the style that Queen Marie Antoinette made so fashionable at the Petit Trianon at Versailles. Flummeries (spiced cream set with calves' feet, hartshorn jelly or isinglass), junkets and syllabubs were made in an elegant chamber lined with Derbyshire alabaster and lit by stained glass.

The Tower of the Winds at Shugborough, Staffordshire, a detail from a watercolour by Moses Griffith, c.1780. The tower had been built twenty years earlier as a banqueting house, and was converted to a dairy in 1805 when the lake was drained

Another fine Georgian dairy is to be found at Uppark in Sussex. Designed by Humphry Repton in the first decade of the 19th century, it backs on to the home farm. As at Shugborough, it is lit by stained glass to filter the light. White Wedgwood tiles edged with twining ivy line the walls, and marble-trimmed slate shelves provide cool surfaces for the flat pans in which the milk was left to separate. This again was a 'fancy dairy', the real work took place next door in the scullery, with its sloping wooden gutter to take water from the pump to the copper, used for washing utensils, scalding cream and warming milk for cheese-making.

The master of Uppark at this time was Sir Harry Fetherstonhaugh. In 1824, still unmarried at the age of seventy, he passed by the dairy one day and heard a girl singing. This was the dairymaid's assistant, Mary Ann Bullock. Sir Harry duly presented himself and asked for her hand in marriage, and Mary Ann Bullock, aged just twenty-one, was sent to Paris to be educated before being married to Sir Harry in September 1825.

One of the most extraordinary dairies in the National Trust's care stands in the grounds of Ham House, Surrey. Here the tiled walls and marble slabs are supported on delicate cows' legs. The Trust is currently restoring this 18th-century phenomenon and hopes to open it to the public.

The dairy at Uppark, Sussex, designed by Humphry Repton. Here worked Mary Ann Bullock, who married Sir Harry Fetherstonhaugh in 1825

Earthenware cow creamer from Fenton House, Hampstead, with an opening in the back for filling, a spout in the form of the mouth, and the curved tail as a handle

Robert Kerr, writing *The Gentleman's House* in 1864, recommended the ideal dairy should be 'a small apartment, ventilated for summer, and supplied with glass inner windows for cold weather'. In the adjoining dairy scullery he advocated a copper, a dresser and benches. Ideally the two rooms should not connect directly, lest heat and steam from the scalding process in the scullery upset the delicate setting processes in the dairy.

Kerr's recommendations are well illustrated by the late Victorian dairy and scullery at Lanhydrock, rebuilt after the fire of 1881. The dairy is provided with ingenious cooling arrangements, whereby water piped from a spring in the hillside flows in a channel around a marble slab in the middle of the room and around slate slabs on its perimeter. The elaborate cold puddings so admired by the Victorians were kept on the marble slab, while cream, butter and milk prepared in the scullery were stored on the slate shelves around the tiled walls. In the scullery next door a scalding range was built on the inner wall of the house, and heated to a gentle temperature by hot water pipes from the boiler-house in the cellar below.

Old habits die hard, and Mrs Beeton's pronouncements on cheese in her *Book of House-hold Management* echo the attitudes of earlier centuries to products of the dairy: 'Cheese, in its commonest shape, is fit only for sedentary people as an after-dinner stimulant, and in very small quantity. Bread and cheese, as a meal, is only fit for soldiers on the march, or labourers in the open air.'

The late 19th-century dairy at Lanhydrock, with marble slabs kept cool by running water

Cleanliness and Decency

To misquote Mark Twain, the report of our ancestors' lack of hygiene is an exaggeration. Of course standards depended on time and place, but in prosperous households valiant efforts were made over the centuries to provide good water supplies, and thus the wherewithal for bathing and lavatories.

The Romans had their hypocausts and aqueducts, the medieval monks their networks of pipes and cisterns, the lords of castles their wells, privy towers and drains. By the late 16th century rotating machines were being used to pump water uphill. At Hardwick Hall in Derbyshire, for instance, a horse-wheel pumped water from a well into a conduit house to the south of the mansion and the water was then piped in lead conduits into the house itself.

Sir Edward Ford is credited with inventing a 'rare engine' in 1656 to raise the waters of the Thames to the highest streets of London, 'to the wonder of all men and the Honour of the Nation'. Sir Edward's grandson, Lord Tankerville, was to use this pumping engine to good effect when he chose to build a fine house high up on the Sussex Downs at Uppark. Pipes of lead and iron took the water up from a spring 350 feet below the house. By the 19th century an indicator on the mantelpiece in the butler's pantry at Uppark measured the level of water stored in roof-top tanks: one of the butler's duties was to keep an eye on the gauge, then regulated by air pressure. Sadly the house's reserves of water did not prove sufficient to prevent it being badly damaged by fire in 1989.

A lead cistern in the inner courtyard at Knole, Kent, decorated with the initials LD for Lionel, 1st Duke of Dorset, and dated 1749

For centuries bathing was a communal activity: medieval manuscripts show two or more people taking a bath in a wooden tub, often with their dinner served on a special tray. In the 17th century Mrs Pepys is recorded by her husband as enjoying the pleasures of the communal bathhouse – the feminine equivalent of a visit to the coffee house.

Taking the waters thereafter became a medicinal as well as a recreational activity and this is reflected in the vogue for country-house bagnios. At Dyrham Park, just outside Bath, Sir William Blaythwayt had a bagnio built in the early 1700s. In a letter to his agent, he records 'preparing to set ye Tile', which may refer to delft tiles, and of soldering sheets of lead to hold hot water. It is thought that the Dyrham bagnio consisted of two rooms, one having a warm bath and shower supplied with water from the kitchen, and the other a cold plunge bath. A spectacular plunge pool can still be seen on the ground floor of Wimpole Hall in Cambridgeshire. Here in the 1790s Sir John Soane put in a bath capable of holding 2,199 gallons of water, heated by a boiler in the basement below.

The bath house at Wimpole Hall, Cambridgeshire. The double staircase sweeps down from the dressing-room to the bath, with a central plinth possibly intended for the statue of a bathing goddess. On the right is a bamboo shower like the one shown in John Leech's cartoon of 1851 (below)

DOMESTIC SANITARY REGULATIONS.

For centuries, private washing facilities meant a basin and ewer in the bedroom or dressing-room, with warm water brought up from the kitchen. In the late 19th century, washstands fitted with taps were introduced. At Cragside Lord Armstrong insisted on the luxury of providing one in every bedroom.

Baths could be taken in front of the dressing-room fire, again with water carried up laboriously by maids and footmen. These baths came in a variety of shapes: shallow saucers, hip baths, and slipper baths – shaped like boots with a tap in the toe, keeping the bather warm in the steam while the floor around remained dry. There is a good example of a slipper bath at Wallington. Showers were also making their appearance. At Wimpole and Erddig there are interesting hand-pumped examples, with a pipe hidden in one of the supports. The water was pumped up to a water tank in the top, and released by pulling a chain that allowed it to pour through a sieve on to the bather (see pages 36 and 37).

Fitted bathrooms with hot and cold water were introduced into country houses from the 1820s, but the supply was not over generous – when Lanhydrock was rebuilt in the 1880s, only one bathroom was provided – and this was for the use of gentlemen rather than ladies. Indeed Lady Fry in the 1920s dismissed bathrooms as 'only for servants'. Perhaps the most functional bathroom – very definitely not for the servants – is to be seen at Castle Drogo in Devon. Designed in the early years of this century by Sir Edwin Lutyens, it boasts a stream-lined enamel bath with five chrome taps on the shower cabinet.

A late 19th-century hip bath and other washing comforts in Captain Shelton's Bedroom, The Argory, County Armagh

Early privies, like baths, were communal affairs: the latrines for the Roman soldiers at Housesteads Fort on Hadrian's Wall; the reredorter for monks over the River Skell at Fountains Abbey in Yorkshire; and garderobes such as the one at Compton Castle in Devon, with seats around a central shaft. William Windham of Felbrigg in Norfolk wrote to his architect, James Paine, in 1752 about a little house by the laundry drying ground: 'How many holes? there must be one for a child; and I would have it as light as possible. There must be a good broad place to set a candle on, and a place to keep paper.' This sort of privy, which would have been furnished with a bucket full of dry earth or cinders to be thrown in after use, was cleared out at regular intervals by the gardeners or 'night-soil' men.

For those who preferred privacy, a chamberpot would be kept under the bed, or a close-stool in the closet. The latter was a box containing a padded seat and a set-in pot. Bess of Hardwick's close-stool, according to the 1601 inventory, was 'blewe cloth sticht with white, with red and black silk fringe'.

The water closet was invented by Sir John Harington, poet and godson of Elizabeth I. In *Metamorphosis of Ajax*, written in 1596 and punning on the word jakes, a privy, he described his creation: a pipe connecting the cistern with the bowl below 'to yield water with a pretty strength when you would let it in'. The vault below would be emptied noon and night – perhaps this explains why his idea was not widely adopted. Only in the 1870s did Harington's vision come to fulfilment with the 'wash down' closet, using a flush of sufficient power to force the contents through the S-bend. These handsome facilities, with their fine mahogany seats and blue and white patterned earthenware, are now the stuff of fond memories.

The King's Closet, Knole, furnished as it would have been in the 17th century. The close-stool, with a red velvet lid, is shown in the right foreground. Originally it would have been kept in the more private 'dark closet' next door

Nurseries

The country-house nursery is a comparatively recent addition to domestic arrange-ments, its heyday being the Victorian and Edwardian years. The late 17th-century inventory for Belton House in Lincolnshire provides tantalising references to what came before. The main nursery was furnished with two four-poster beds, one with hangings of crimson mohair, the other curtained in grey angora. The little nursery had a bedstead of purple curtains and a cradle complete with feather mattress and pillows. Richness of texture was clearly much more important than practicality.

As the concept of childhood developed, so children were expected to spend more time in the nursery. In the early 19th century nurseries were situated far away from the hub of the household, often in attics. Later, they were placed nearer to the mother's boudoir, perhaps following the example of Queen Victoria. At Lanhydrock the Trust has just restored the nurseries, built in the 1880s and with easy access to Lord and Lady Clifden's rooms. Late-Victorian examples, such as those at Lanhydrock and at Wight-wick Manor in the West Midlands, were divided into day and night nurseries. In the day nursery children played and took their meals. In the night nursery the younger children slept, moving into other rooms as they grew older.

The day nursery at Wightwick Manor, West Midlands, filled with toys and games. The curtains, screen and cushions are designs by Charles Voysey, 1929, 'The House that Jack Built' and 'Alice in Wonderland'

The country-house nursery was presided over by the nurse or nanny, a figure who could wield great influence over her charges. Winston Churchill was devoted to his nanny, Mrs Elizabeth Ann Everest, finding the human contact with her that he could not enjoy with his mother, the beauty Jennie, who was much in society. George Curzon, brought up in the nursery at Kedleston Hall in Derbyshire in the 1860s, had a very different experience with his nanny, Miss Paraman. After Curzon's death in 1925, handwritten notes were discovered detailing the terrible times he and his siblings had experienced under her regime: 'In her savage moments she was a brutal and vindictive tyrant; and I have often thought since that she must have been insane. She persecuted and beat us in the most cruel way and established over us a system of terrorism so complete that not one of us ever mustered up the courage to tell our father or mother.'

Nanny would often be assisted by nursery maids, and in larger establishments there would be a footman who waited mainly on the nursery. The food, often specially prepared, was intended to be light and nutritious, but memories often dwell upon its awfulness. Anthea Mander Lahr recalled her childhood at Wightwick in the *National Trust Magazine* in 1992: 'Frugal meals consisted of eggs, baked beans, cheese dreams, roes and creamed haddock (my favourite) . . . . My brother John was made to sit for hours, chewing the cud on cold, unappetising food. No wonder so many of the children from these nurseries found drink more palatable and comforting.'

The night nursery at Lanhydrock, with cots and beds for the younger children. Nanny would have slept in the bedroom opening off to the left of the fireplace

The fireplace in the night nursery at Wightwick, with tiles made by Minton to designs by Ellen Houghton of the days of the week. The printed frieze of birds and animals was designed in 1908 by the sporting artist, Cecil Aldin

When children grew out of the nursery, so they moved on to the schoolroom. For their first years of schooling, boys and girls were taught by a governess, but while sons then went on to a private tutor or away to boarding school, daughters almost always remained in the schoolroom. Theresa Parker, writing to her sister Anne Robinson from Saltram in Devon observed, 'Mothers must give up their boys, but keep girls constantly under their eye'. In fact Theresa died in November 1775, less than two months after giving birth to her daughter, also called Theresa. Anne was left to look after Theresa and a three-year-old son, Jack. Jack was sent off at the age of seven to attend Dr Kyte's School at Hammersmith, then just outside London, but his sister Theresa remained at Saltram with a French governess, who turned out to be a great success. Anne wrote enthusiastically: 'I flatter myself we have got a treasure in her as Governess, she is perfectly good natured, well-behaved, modest and seems sensible . . . . Her not speaking English I look upon as her greatest advantage, as she has no temptation to mix with other servants and be spoiled . . . .'

The ambiguous status of governesses in the strict hierarchy of country houses continued to cause problems right through to this century. Ursula Wyndham, brought up at Petworth and Florence Court in Northern Ireland in the 1920s, wrote of her governesses in her autobiography, *Astride the Wall*: '. . . they were totally isolated. Parents left them in sole command of the schoolroom and treated them with the distant civility they extended to domestic staff. The governess was intent on proving her gentility, but nobody was interested.' Jane Eyre would have sympathised.

The nursery suite at Lanhydrock was completed by a special bathroom designed to cater for small children

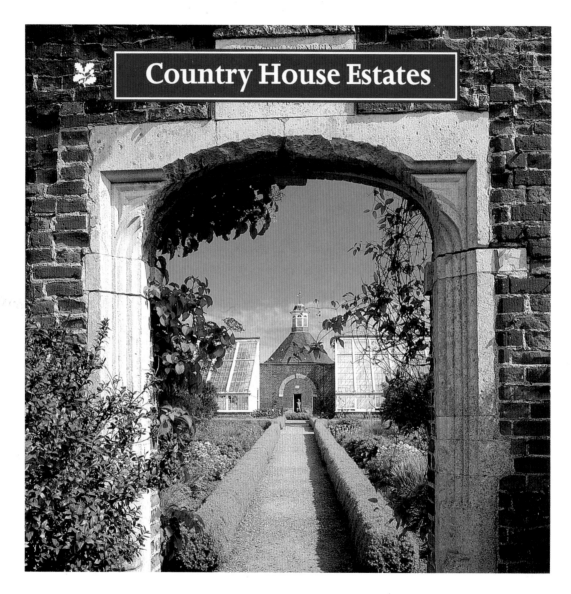

Country House Estates

A companion to this booklet, concentrating on the realm of the land agent, the woodmen and gamekeepers, the stable lads and blacksmiths, the gardener and the laundrymaid.